★
ICONS

MIAMI STYLE

MIAM

Exteriors   Interiors

STYLE
Details

PHOTOS **Eric Laignel**
PRODUCTION **Patricia Parinejad**
EDITOR **Angelika Taschen**

TASCHEN
HONGKONG KÖLN LONDON LOS ANGELES MADRID PARIS TOKYO

Front Cover: Purist pool design: at Tom Healys and Fred Hochbergs house on the Sunset Islands.
Couverture: Piscine au design puriste : chez Tom Healy et Fred Hochberg aux îles Sunset.
Umschlagvorderseite: Puristisches Pooldesign: Bei Tom Healy und Fred Hochberg auf den Sunset Islands.

Back Cover: Chill out: panorama view at Carlos Cisneros.
Dos de Couverture: Chill out : place pour voir le panorama, chez Carlos Cisneros.
Umschlagrückseite: Chill out: Panoramaplatz bei Carlos Cisneros.

Also available from TASCHEN:

Miami Interiors
320 pages
ISBN-10: 3-8228-1655-8
ISBN-13: 978-3-8228-1655-4

To stay informed about upcoming TASCHEN titles, please request our magazine
at www.taschen.com/magazine or write to TASCHEN, Hohenzollernring 53, D-50672 Cologne,
Germany, contact@taschen.com, Fax: +49-221-254919. We will be happy to send you a free copy
of our magazine which is filled with information about all of our books.

Concept and editing by Angelika Taschen, Berlin
Layout and project management by Stephanie Bischoff, Cologne
Texts by Christiane Reiter, Hamburg
Lithography by Thomas Grell, Cologne
English translation by Pauline Cumbers, Frankfurt am Main
French translation by Anne Charrière, Croissy/Seine

Printed in Italy
ISBN-10: 3-8228-2570-0
ISBN-13: 978-3-8228-2570-9

CONTENTS SOMMAIRE INHALT

Visiting Miami for the first time and driving along Ocean Drive from South Beach, you are served a cream-cake and soft-ice version of modern America. Art-Deco buildings in flamingo pink, sunflower yellow and azure blue; sparkling neon signs on the facades like fashionable jewelry at night, and in front of the doors palms soaring upwards on slightly curving trunks. About 800 of these paradisiacal, pastel-shaded buildings make Miami the world's most important Art-Deco city and provide the backdrop for fashion shootings, advertising spots and TV series – including that all-time favorite "Miami Vice", which was broadcast in more than 130 countries and through which Don Johnson made the combination of colored jacket and T-shirt socially acceptable. Miami has sex appeal and holds the promise of life on the sunny side – not only for locals and tourists, but also for immigrants: Nowhere else in America are there as many Cubans, and they give the city a Caribbean-Spanish flair. Be it in Little Havana, the Mediterranean-tinged Coconut Grove,

MIAMI NICE

La première impression de Miami, quand on prend la route de l'Océan à South Beach, est celle d'une Amérique moderne, version tarte à la crème et glace à l'italienne : des bâtiments Art Déco en rose flamant, jaune soleil et bleu azur ; sur les façades, des caractères au néon qui flamboient, la nuit, comme des bijoux de pacotille ; et devant les portes, des palmiers qui se dressent vers le ciel sur des troncs légèrement arqués. Avec environ 800 maisons paradisiaques aux teintes pastel, Miami est la plus importante ville Art Déco du monde et le décor rêvé des photos de mode, des spots publicitaires et des séries télévisées. C'est toute l'atmosphère de la série culte « Deux flics à Miami », diffusée dans plus de 130 pays, où la combinaison T-shirt plus veston coloré portée par Don Johnson avait conquis le jet-set. Vibrante, sensuelle, Miami promet une vie radieuse à ses habitants, à ses touristes, et même à ses immigrés. Aucun autre lieu d'Amérique n'abrite autant de Cubains. La ville leur doit son ambiance hispano-caribéenne. Que ce soit à « Little Havana », au « Coconut Grove » avec sa note méditerranéenne, dans les

Wer zum ersten Mal in Miami ist und über den Ocean Drive von South Beach fährt, bekommt eine Cremeschnitten- und Softeisversion des modernen Amerikas serviert. Art-Déco-Gebäude in Flamingopink, Sonnengelb und Azurblau; an der Fassade Neonschriftzüge, die nachts wie Modeschmuck funkeln, und vor der Tür Palmen, die auf leicht gebogenen Stämmen in den Himmel ragen. Rund 800 dieser Paradiesbauten in Pastell machen Miami zur wichtigsten Art-Déco-Stadt der Welt und bilden die Kulisse für Modeshootings, Werbespots und TV-Serien – darunter der Quotenhit »Miami Vice«, der in mehr als 130 Ländern ausgestrahlt wurde und mit dem Don Johnson die Kombination aus buntem Jackett und T-Shirt salonfähig machte. Miami hat Sexappeal und verspricht ein Dasein auf der Sonnenseite – nicht nur Einheimischen und Touristen, sondern auch Einwanderern: Nirgendwo sonst in Amerika leben so viele Kubaner wie hier und verleihen der Stadt karibisch-spanisches Flair. Ob in »Little Havana«, dem mediterran angehauchten »Coconut Grove«, den Venetian

the Venetian Islands or in South Beach, Miami has an international cheerful style and is marked by the proximity of the sea (the name comes from the Indian word "Mayaimi", meaning great water). Many of its buildings are reminiscent of summer houses and beach pavilions, painted in white and blue with clear lines and providing panoramic views of swimming pools, tropical gardens or the Atlantic. Design classics give the interiors a touch of sophistication – be that an armchair by Mies van der Rohe, a sofa by Arne Jacobsen or a chair by Eero Saarinen. The carefully and lavishly renovated Art-Deco houses are more glamorously luxurious: With their wrought-iron railings, slim-line columns and chandeliers, they celebrate one of the 20th century's most beautiful styles, the Eden Roc Hotel first and foremost. And if you want to experience Miami from its humorously colorful, low-budget side, you need only travel to Key Biscayne or Stiltsville, where all you require is some wood and a splash of paint to achieve a modicum of happiness.

îles vénitiennes ou à South Beach, Miami affiche un style international joyeux, marqué par sa proximité avec la mer (d'ailleurs son nom, dérivé du mot indien « Mayaimi », signifie « Grande eau »). Beaucoup de maisons sont construites dans un style villégiature ou pavillon de plage, avec des lignes claires, des tons blancs et bleus, et une vision panoramique sur des piscines, des jardins tropicaux ou l'Atlantique. Les grands classiques du design – fauteuil de Mies van der Rohe, sofa d'Arne Jacobsen ou chaises d'Eero Saarinen – confèrent à ces intérieurs un air très sophistiqué. Dans un charme plus glamoureux, les belles demeures Art Déco, rénovées avec soin et à grands frais, l'hôtel Eden Roc en tête, célèbrent avec leurs rampes en fer forgé, leurs colonnes élancées et leurs lustres de cristal, l'un des plus beaux styles du XXᵉ siècle. Et celui qui veut se plonger dans la vie riante et colorée des quartiers moins fortunés n'a qu'à se rendre à la Baie de Biscayne ou à Stiltsville, où quelques planches de bois et un peu de couleur suffisent à faire le bonheur.

Islands oder eben in South Beach: Miami besitzt einen internationalen, fröhlichen Stil und ist von der Nähe zum Meer geprägt (nicht umsonst stammt sein Name vom indianischen »Mayaimi«, was »Großes Wasser« bedeutet). Viele Bauten erinnern an Sommerhäuser und Strandpavillons, sind in Weiß und Blau sowie in klaren Linien gehalten und eröffnen Panoramablicke auf Pools, tropische Gärten oder den Atlantik. Designklassiker lassen die Interiors sehr sophisticated wirken – sei es ein Sessel von Mies van der Rohe, ein Sofa von Arne Jacobsen oder ein Stuhl von Eero Saarinen. Üppiger und glamouröser geben sich die sorgfältig und kostspielig renovierten Art-Déco-Häuser: das Eden Roc Hotel an der Spitze, zelebrieren sie mit schmiedeeisernen Geländern, schlanken Säulen und Kristallleuchtern einen der schönsten Stile des 20. Jahrhunderts. Und wer Miami von seiner lustig-bunten Low-Budget-Seite erleben möchte, muss nur nach Key Biscayne oder Stiltsville fahren, wo man zum kleinen Glück nicht mehr als Holz und ein bisschen Farbe braucht.

"...The sea was glistening brightly, almost painfully, as if millions of silver coins had been strewn..."

Stephen Grave, *Miami Vice*. *The Florida Burn*

«...La mer scintillait claire, presque douloureusement, comme si des millions de pièces d'argent avaient été semées...»

Stephen Grave, *Miami Vice*. *Presses de la cité*

»...Das Meer schimmerte hell, fast schmerzhaft, so als wären Millionen Silbermünzen ausgestreut worden...«

Stephen Grave, *Miami Vice*. *Heißes Pflaster Florida*

EXTERIORS

Extérieurs   Aussichten

10/11 Colored reflections on water: Miami skyline by night. *Réflexions de couleurs sur l'eau : la ligne des gratte-ciels de Miami, la nuit.* Farbreflexe auf dem Wasser: Die Skyline von Miami bei Nacht.

12/13 A blowing blue: the Colony Hotel on the legendary Ocean Drive. *Sur un fond bleu lumineux : l'hôtel Colony sur le légendaire Ocean Drive.* Leuchtend blau: Das Colony Hotel am legendären Ocean Drive.

14/15 Ready for a cruise: in front of the Avalon Hotel in South Beach. *Élégante et fend-le-vent : devant l'hôtel Avalon, à South Beach.* Flotter Flitzer: Vor dem Avalon Hotel in South Beach.

16/17 50s style: the Eden Roc Hotel, 1956, by Morris Lapidus. *Années 50 : l'hôtel Eden Roc, construit en 1956 par Morris Lapidus.* Aus den Fifties: Das Eden Roc Hotel, 1956 von Morris Lapidus erbaut.

18/19 60s style: former home of TV-star Jackie Gleason. *Années 60 : l'ancienne maison d'une star de la télévision, Jackie Gleason.* Aus den Sixties: Das ehemalige Haus von TV-Star Jackie Gleason.

20/21 Apartments with a view: the now listed Helen Mar building. *Appartements avec vue panoramique : dans l'immeuble d'Helen Mar, inscrit aux monuments historiques.* Apartments mit Ausblick: Im denkmalgeschützten Helen-Mar-Gebäude.

22/23 Post-Deco style: bungalow owned by Leticia and Michele Grendene. *Dans le style post-déco : le bungalow de Leticia et Michele Grendene.* Im Post-Deco-Stil: Der Bungalow von Leticia und Michele Grendene.

24/25 Taking a dive: the Grendenes's son and dog go swimming. *Elan : le fils et le chien des Grendene au bord de l'élément humide.* Auf dem Sprung: Sohn und Hund der Grendenes fast im nassen Element.

26/27 In the green: Stephen Montifiore's summer house. *En pleine nature : la maison estivale de Stephen Montifiore.* Mitten im Grünen: Das sommerliche Haus von Stephen Montifiore.

28/29 Long Lafco table: at Tom Healy's and Fred Hochberg pool on the Sunset Islands. *Longue table Lafco : au bord de la piscine de Tom Healy et Fred Hochberg aux îles Sunset.* Lange Lafco-Tafel: An Tom Healys und Fred Hochberg Pool auf den Sunset Islands.

30/31 Huge palm pot by Philippe Starck: on Christian Kolm's terrace. *Méga pots de palmiers de Philippe Starck : sur la terrasse de Christian Kolm.* Mega-Palmentöpfe von Philippe Starck: Auf Christian Kolms Terrasse.

32/33 Purist pool design: at Carlos Cisneros's home on Palm Island. *Piscine au design puriste : chez Carlos Cisneros sur Palm Island.* Puristisches Pooldesign: Bei Carlos Cisneros auf Palm Island.

34/35 A dream day bed: panorama view at Carlos Cisneros's pool. *Un rêve de lit de jour : pour voir le panorama, chez Carlos Cisneros.* Traumhaftes Tagesbett: Panoramaplatz bei Carlos Cisneros.

36/37 Ink-blue sea: in front of Kent Karlock's house on the Venetian Islands. *Mer bleu d'encre : devant la maison de Kent Karlock sur les îles vénitiennes.* Tintenblaues Meer: Vor Kent Karlocks Haus auf den Venetian Islands.

38/39 On stilts: Stiltsville, 1,2 miles south of Cape Florida. *Construction sur pilotis : à Stiltsville, deux kilomètres au sud du Cap Floride.* Auf Stelzen gebaut: Stiltsville, zwei Kilometer südlich von Cape Florida.

40/41 Colorfully out of kilter: Jimbo's hut in Key Biscayne. *La couleur prime : hutte de guingois, hutte de Jimbo à Key Biscayne.* Hauptsache, bunt: Jimbos windschiefe Hütte in Key Biscayne.

42/43 A classically stylish beach house: at Pierre Casteleyn's and Max Griffin's. *Maison de plage classique et de style : chez Pierre Casteleyn et Max Griffin.* Ein klassisches Strandhaus mit Stil: Bei Pierre Casteleyn und Max Griffin.

44/45 A shady spot: at Ellen and Ian Ball's home in the idyllic Coconut Grove. *Coin d'ombre : chez Ellen et Ian Ball, dans la petite commune idyllique de Coconut Grove.* Schattenplatz: Bei Ellen und Ian Ball im idyllischen Coconut Grove.

"…The room was plastered white and quite bare, apart from a couple of modern lithographs…"

Max Allan Collins, *CSI: Miami. Florida Getaway*

«…La pièce était crépie de blanc et assez nue, hormis quelques lithographies modernes…»

Max Allan Collins, *Les Experts, CSI: Miami*

»…Der Raum war weiß verputzt und ziemlich kahl, abgesehen von einigen modernen Lithografien…«

Max Allan Collins, *CSI: Miami. Fluchtpunkt Florida*

INTERIORS

Intérieurs   Einsichten

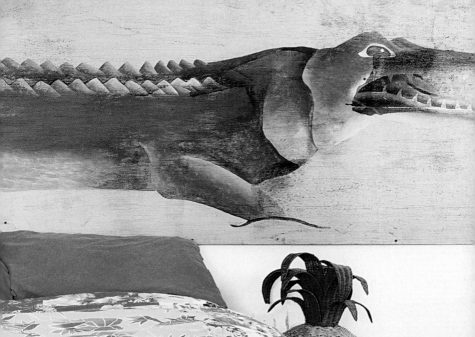

50/51 Liz Taylor and Frank Sinatra once stayed here: at Eden Roc. *L'Eden Roc : Liz Taylor et Frank Sinatra y ont séjourné.* Wo schon Liz Taylor und Frank Sinatra zu Gast waren: Das Eden Roc.

52/53 Art Deco par excellence: a penthouse in the Helen Mar building. *Art Déco superbe : dans un penthouse de l'immeuble Helen Mar.* Glanzvolles Art Déco: In einem Penthouse des Helen-Mar-Buildings.

54/55 A touch of Egypt: pillars of milky glass, nickel and brass. *Un air égyptien : colonnes d'entrée en verre dépoli, nickel et laiton.* Ägyptisch angehaucht: Eingangssäulen aus Milchglas, Nickel und Messing.

56/57 The perfect window seat: in an octagonal building by Gene E. Baylis. *Place fantastique près de la fenêtre : dans une construction octogonale de Gene E. Baylis.* Fantastischer Fensterplatz: In einem Achteck-Bau von Gene E. Baylis.

58/59 Mix: a "Lily" chair, an Africa stool and chairs by Mies van der Rohe. *Métissage : chaise « Lily », tabourets africains et fauteuil Mies van der Rohe.* Mix: Stuhl »Lily«, afrikanische Hocker und Sessel von Mies van der Rohe.

60/61 Splashes of color: Andy Warhol's "Flowers" at the home of Tui Pranich. *Touches florales colorées : « Flowers » d'Andy Warhol dans la maison de Tui Pranich.* Floreale Farbtupfer: Andy Warhols »Flowers« im Haus von Tui Pranich.

62/63 Favorite painting: "Eric" by Robert Longo; at the home of Tui Pranich. *Tableau préféré : « Eric » de Robert Longo ; également chez Tui Pranich.* Lieblingsbild: »Eric« von Robert Longo; ebenfalls bei Tui Pranich.

64/65 Basically white with a touch of Feng Shui: at Tui Pranich's home. *Blanc en couleur fondamentale et philosophie Feng Shui : chez Tui Pranich.* Grundfarbe Weiß und Feng-Shui-Philosophie: Bei Tui Pranich.

66/67 Safari sofa and "Patroclo" lamp: at Kim & Al Eiber's house. *Canapé Safari et lampe « Patroclo » : dans la maison de Kim et Al Eiber.* Safari-Sofa und »Patroclo«-Lampe: Im Haus von Kim & Al Eiber.

68/69 A foot in: colorful design by Gaetano Pesce at the Eiber's house. *Un pied monumental : design multicolore de Gaetano Pesce chez les Eiber.* Auf großem Fuß: Buntes Design von Gaetano Pesce bei den Eibers.

70/71 Florida colors: the "Miami Sound" shelving is also by Pesce. *Aux couleurs de la Floride : l'étagère « Miami Sound » est elle aussi une œuvre de Pesce.* Die Farben Floridas: Auch das Regal »Miami Sound« stammt von Pesce.

72/73 A bright atmosphere: at the home of Tom Healy and Fred Hochberg, designed by Alison Spear. *Ambiance claire : dans la maison de Tom Healy et Fred Hochberg, aménagée par Alison Spear.* Helles Ambiente: Im Haus von Tom Healy und Fred Hochberg, gestaltet von Alison Spear.

74/75 That certain something: a crystal chandelier above a table by Monica Armani. *Extra étincelant : lampe de cristal au-dessus d'une table de Monica Armani.* Glitzerndes Extra: Kristalllampe über einem Tisch von Monica Armani.

76/77 Photos of family and friends: at the home of Leticia and Michele Grendene. *Photos de famille et d'amis : chez Leticia et Michele Grendene.* Fotos von Familie und Freunden: Bei Leticia und Michele Grendene.

78/79 Clear lines: the Grendenes's bedroom in Rivo Alto. *Lignes claires : la chambre à coucher des Grendene, à Rivo Alto.* Klare Linien: Das Schlafzimmer der Grendenes in Rivo Alto.

80/81 Curvy: Verner Panton chairs at the home of Kent Karlock. *Courbes élancées : chaises Verner Panton dans la maison de Kent Karlock.* Schön geschwungen: Verner Panton-Stühle im Haus von Kent Karlock.

82/83 Spacious: Karlock's bungalow is designed by Rolando Llanes. *Spacieux : le bungalow de Karlock est une construction de Rolando Llanes.* Raum und Weite: Karlocks Bungalow ist ein Bau von Rolando Llanes.

84/85 Classics: Eero Saarinen's "Tulip" chairs around Kent Karlock's dining table. *Des classiques : chaises « tulipe » d'Eero Saarinen entourant la table à manger de Kent Karlock.* Klassiker: Eero Saarinens »Tulip«-Stühle rund um Kent Karlocks Esstisch.

86/87 Quartet: four "July" chairs in the town house of two contemporary artists. *Quatuor : quatre chaises « Juli » dans la maison de ville de deux artistes contemporains.* Quartett: Vier »Juli«-Stühle im Stadthaus zweier Gegenwartskünstler.

88/89 Subtle shades: leather stools beside a "Womb Chair" in rust red. *Couleurs nobles : tabouret de cuir à côté d'une chaise « Womb », teinte rouille.* Edle Farben: Lederhocker neben einem »Womb Chair« in Rostrot.

90/91 Retro elegance: armchair by Gio Ponti in Jiska Timmer and Massimo Barracca's villa. *Rétro-élégance : fauteuil de Gio Ponti dans la villa de Jiska Timmer et Massimo Barracca.* Retro-Eleganz: Sessel von Gio Ponti in Jiska Timmer und Massimo Barraccas Villa.

92/93 Europe in 1937: original map on parchment in Timmer's and Massimo Barracca's house. *Europe année 1937: carte originale sur parchemin dans la maison Timmer et Barracca.* Europa anno 1937: Originalkarte auf Pergament in Timmers und Barraccas Haus.

94/95 Green oasis: bath- and bedroom in the Keenen/Riley home of Carlos Cisneros. *Oasis verte : salle de bains et lit dans la maison Keenen/Riley de Carlos Cisneros.* Grüne Oase: Bad und Bett im Keenen/Riley-Haus von Carlos Cisneros.

96/97 Hovering: cabinet and staircase, also in Cisneros's house. *Presque flottants : console et escalier, également chez Cisneros.* Scheinbar schwebend: Konsole und Treppe, ebenfalls bei Cisneros.

98/99 "Burning bushes": artworks in the apartment of Michele Oka Doner. *« Buissons ardents »: œuvres d'art dans l'appartement de Michele Oka Doner.* »Burning bushes«: Kunstwerke im Apartment von Michele Oka Doner.

100/101 Ancient item: stage set from Shakespeare's "Tempest". *Bijou antique : décors de théâtre pour la pièce de Shakespeare « La Tempête ».* Antikes Schmuckstück: Bühnenbild aus Shakespeares »Der Sturm«.

102/103 Art-Deco lobby in typical shades: Craig Eberhardt's house. *Hall art-déco dans des couleurs typiques : maison de Craig Eberhardt.* Art-Déco-Lobby in typischen Farben: Im Haus von Craig Eberhardt.

104/105 The former dance hall: seven 1959 crystal chandeliers. *Dans l'ancienne salle de danse : sept lustres de cristal de 1959.* Im ehemaligen Tanzsaal: Sieben Kristallleuchter aus dem Jahr 1959.

106/107 Disco fever: Craig Eberhardt's red bar with Memphis-style stools. *Fièvre disco : bar rouge de Craig Eberhardt avec tabourets style Memphis.* Discofieber: Craig Eberhardts rote Bar mit Hockern im Memphis-Stil.

108/109 Quite a collection: Suzanne Lipschutz's Spanish-inspired house. *Collection disparate : dans la maison de Suzanne Lipschutz, d'inspiration espagnole.* Sammelsurium: Im spanisch inspirierten Haus von Suzanne Lipschutz.

110/111 Ornamental: colorful tiles in Carlos Alves's kitchen. *Bijoux : carreaux de cuisine colorés de Carlos Alves de Cuba.* Schmuckstücke: Bunte Küchenkacheln von Carlos Alves aus Kuba.

112/113 Highly personal: a Cuban lady's apartment in the Art-Deco quarter. *Très personnel : appartement d'une Cubaine, dans le quartier Art Déco.* Ganz persönlich: Das Apartment einer Kubanerin im Art-Déco-Viertel.

114/115 Like a chapel: Steven Giles and Bruce Cannella's living room. *Comme une chapelle : dans le séjour de Steven Giles et Bruce Cannella.* Wie eine Kapelle: Im Wohnzimmer von Steven Giles und Bruce Cannella.

116/117 Cosy: Jean-Yves Legrand's dining room on Normandy Isle. *Confortable : salle à manger de Jean-Yves Legrand sur l'île Normandy.* Gemütlich: Esszimmer von Jean-Yves Legrand auf der Normandy Isle.

118/119 On the Keys: Carmen Velasco's pretty beach pavilion. *Dans les Keys : le joli pavillon de plage de Carmen Velasco.* In den Keys gelegen: Der hübsche Strandpavillon von Carmen Velasco.

120/121 Maritime accessories: around a Modénature table. *Accessoires maritimes : tout autour de la table ronde de Modénature.* Maritime Accessoires: Rund um den runden Tisch von Modénature.

122/123 Art by Marcel Warrand: at Pierre Casteleyn and Max Griffin's bar. *Art de Marcel Warrand : décoration pour le bar de Pierre Casteleyn et Max Griffin.* Kunst von Marcel Warrand: An der Bar von Pierre Casteleyn und Max Griffin.

124/125 Center point: glass shower in Casteleyn's and Griffin's bedroom. *Au centre : douche de verre dans la chambre à coucher de Casteleyn et Griffin.* Zentrales Element: Gläserne Dusche im Schlafzimmer von Casteleyn und Griffin.

126/127 Prominent: rattan 1960 furniture and pink "Butterfly". *Mis en scène : mobilier en rotin des années 60 et « papillon » rose.* In Szene gesetzt: Rattanmöbel aus den 1960ern und pinker »Butterfly«.

128/129 Peaceful refuge: Tamara Hendershot's wooden house in Little Haiti. *Refuge paisible : la maison en bois de Tamara Hendershot à Little Haïti.* Ruhiges Refugium: Tamara Hendershots Holzhaus in Little Haiti.

130/131 Lime green: kitchen personally decorated with glass stones from Italy. *Vert citron : cuisine construite par l'habitant, aux carreaux de verre d'Italie.* Limonengrün: Die selbstgebaute Küche mit Glassteinen aus Italien.

132/133 Imaginative: Art-Deco villa of Brian Antoni in Miami. *Univers fantastique : villa Art Déco l'originale, de Brian Antoni à Miami.* Fantasiewelt: Die originelle Art-Déco-Villa von Brian Antoni in Miami.

134/135 Extravagant framework: once a setting for Helmut Newton. *Cadre extravagant : la maison a déjà servi de décor à Helmut Newton.* Extravaganter Rahmen: Das Haus war schon Kulisse für Helmut Newton.

136/137 A gripping ad: Brian Antoni's bizarre bedroom decoration. *Publicité mordante : décor grotesque de chambre à coucher chez Brian Antoni.* Werbung mit Biss: Skurriler Schlafzimmerschmuck bei Brian Antoni.

138/139 Welcome aboard: in Stiltsville, founded by a fisherman. *Bienvenu à bord : à Stiltsville, lieu fondé jadis par un pêcheur.* Willkommen an Bord: In Stiltsville, einst von einem Fischer gegründet.

140/141 Creative chaos: in Jimbo's fishermen's huts in Key Biscayne. *Chaos créatif : dans les cabanes de pêcheurs de Jimbo à Key Biscayne.* Kreatives Chaos: In den Fischerhütten von Jimbo in Key Biscayne.

"…The carpet was deep purple, and the violet velvet curtains took up the color with undiminished force…"

Charles Willeford, *Miami Blues*

«…La moquette était d'un pourpre profond, les rideaux de velours violets en absorbaient la couleur avec une violence irrépressible…»

Charles Willeford, *Miami Blues*

»…Der Teppichboden war von tiefem Purpurrot, und die violetten Samtvorhänge nahmen die Farbe mit unverminderter Wucht auf…«

Charles Willeford, *Miami Blues*

DETAILS

Détails   Details

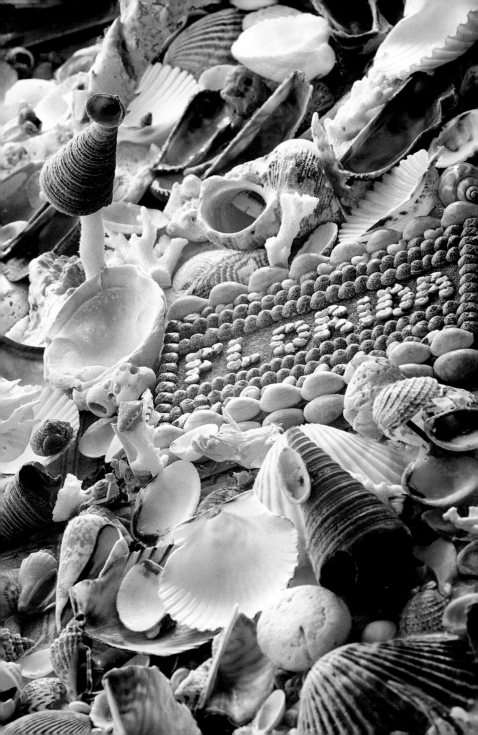

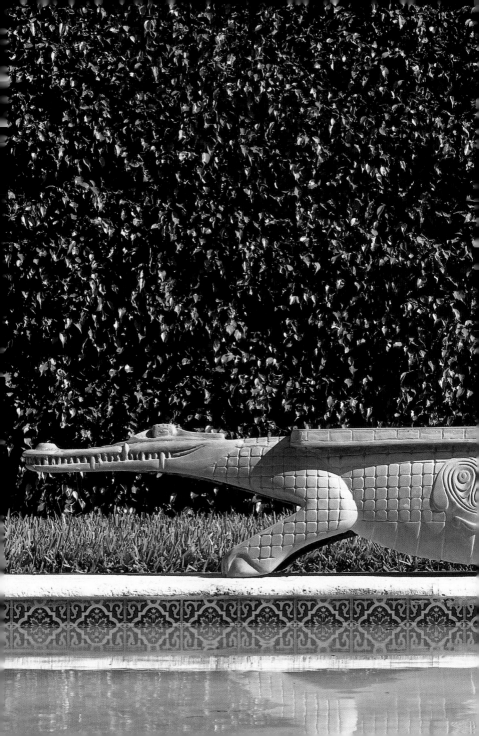

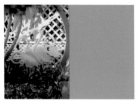 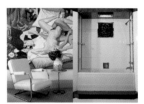

148 Pretty in Pink: flamingos, ubiquitous symbol of Miami. *Couleur intense : les flamants roses, emblème omniprésent de Miami.* Pretty in Pink: Flamingos, allgegenwärtige Wahrzeichen von Miami.

150 Exposed: artwork and armchair at Brian Antoni's in South Beach. *A nu : œuvre d'art et fauteuil par Brian Antoni à South Beach.* Unverhüllt: Kunstwerk und Sessel bei Brian Antoni in South Beach.

151 Bathed in color: Brian Antoni's Art-Deco bathroom. *Plongée dans la couleur : la salle de bains Art Déco de Brian Antoni.* In Farbe getaucht: Brian Antonis Art-Déco-Badezimmer.

153 Awfully nice: Brian Antoni's collection of "ugly" portraits. *Joliment laid : la collection des « vilains » portraits de Brian Antoni.* Hübsch hässlich: Brian Antonis Sammlung »unschöner« Portraits.

154 Table decoration: dishes in the original Florida look. *Décor de table : vaisselle dans le style natif de Floride.* Tischschmuck: Geschirr im originalen Florida-Look.

155 A clear distinction: toilet doors in Stiltsville. *Séparation franche : portes de toilette à Stiltsville.* Klare Trennung: Toilettentüren in Stiltsville.

157 Wreaked: a film-worthy Key Biscayne scene. *Carcasse : dans le décor cinématographique de Key Biscayne.* Zu Schrott gefahren: In der filmreifen Kulisse von Key Biscayne.

158 You've got mail: a typical American mailbox. *Vous avez du courrier : boîte à lettres américaine typique.* You've got mail: Typisch amerikanischer Briefkasten.

159 Directions: signs in front of Jimbo's dwelling. *Orientation : panneaux indicateurs devant l'habitation de Jimbo.* Auf den Weg gebracht: Hinweisschilder vor Jimbos Behausung.

161 Beach souvenirs: shells in a Cuban lady's apartment. *Souvenirs de la plage : coquillages dans l'appartement d'une dame cubaine.* Strand-Souvenirs: Muscheln im Apartment einer kubanischen Lady.

162 Stability: lamp with the flair of yesteryear. *Stabilité : lampe aux accents d'époques révolues.* Standfest: Lampe mit dem Flair vergangener Zeiten.

163 A fleeting gaze: portrait of a lady surrounded by flowers. *L'espace d'un instant : portrait de femme orné de fleurs.* Nur ein Augenblick: Blumengeschmücktes Frauenporträt.

165 The blue hour: Gio Ponti armchair, 1949/50. *Pour une pause bleue : fauteuil Gio Ponti des années 1949/50.* Für die blaue Pause: Gio-Ponti-Sessel aus den Jahren 1949/50.

166 Herald of Pop: "Marshmallow" sofa at the home of Stephen Montifiore. *Précurseur du pop : canapé « Marshmallow » par Stephen Montifiore.* Vorbote des Pop: »Marshmallow«-Sofa bei Stephen Montifiore.

167 Matching tones: pictures and chairs at Brian Antoni's place. *Ton sur ton : dessins et chaises de Brian Antoni.* Ton in Ton: Bilder und Stühle bei Brian Antoni.

168 View of nature: from Tui Pranich's living room. *Vue sur la nature : depuis le séjour de Tui Pranich.* Blick in die Natur: Von Tui Pranichs Wohnzimmer aus.

170 Time for design: the "Swan" sofa by Arne Jacobsen. *L'heure du design : canapé « Cygne » d'Arne Jacobsen.* Zeit für Design: Das »Swan«-Sofa von Arne Jacobsen.

171 To the second: clock from Stephen Montifiore's collection. *Précise à la seconde : horloge de la collection de Stephen Montifiore.* Sekundengenau: Uhr aus der Sammlung von Stephen Montifiore.

173 Striking color combination: Mario Cader-Frech's town house. *Combinaison de couleurs réussie : dans la maison de ville de Mario Cader-Frech.* Wirkungsvolle Farbkombination: Im Stadthaus von Mario Cader-Frech.

174 Animal presence: cuddly leopard and parrot picture at Craig Eberhardt's. *Bêtement bien : léopard en peluche et tableau de perroquets chez Craig Eberhardt.* Tierisch gut: Plüschleopard und Papageien-Bild bei Craig Eberhardt.

175 Feline curiosity: Eberhardt's cat in an Art-Deco ambience. *Bêtement intéressant : le chat d'Eberhardt au milieu du décor Art Déco.* Tierisch interessant: Eberhardts Kater mitten im Art-Déco-Ambiente.

177 Former display window piece: a 1930s seahorse. *Décoration de vitrine reclassée : hippocampe des années 1930.* Ausrangierter Schaufenster-Schmuck: Seepferd aus den 1930ern.

178 With a bite: stone crocodile bench at Susan and John Rothchild's pool. *Dents serrées : banc de piscine crocodile en pierre, chez Susan et John Rothchild.* Bissfest: Steinerne Kroko-Poolbank bei Susan und John Rothchild.

179 Legend on Miami beach: Morris Lapidus's Eden Roc Hotel. *Edifice légendaire sur la plage de sable de Miami : l'hôtel Eden Roc de Morris Lapidus.* Legende am Sandstrand von Miami: Morris Lapidus' Eden Roc Hotel.

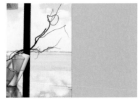

180 Imaginative shapes: branches in a frosted glass vase *Formes créatives : branches dans un vase en verre opalin.* Fantasievolle Formen: Zweige in einer Vase aus Milchglas.

182 The 1940s: a ceramic pot filled with aloe vera. *Œuvre des années 40 : une coupe en céramique, remplie d'aloe vera.* Aus den 1940er-Jahren: Eine Keramikschale, gefüllt mit Aloe Vera.

183 Filigree artworks: the "burning bushes" by Michele Oka Doner. *Tout en filigrane : les « buissons ardents » de Michele Oka Doner.* Filigrane Kunstwerke: Die »burning bushes« von Michele Oka Doner.

185 A still-life in oceanic blue: at Michele Oka Doner's. *Nature morte dans les tons de l'océan : chez Michele Oka Doner.* Stillleben in den Tönen des Ozeans: Bei Michele Oka Doner.

186 Secure: Brian Antoni's villa behind wrought-iron gates. *Sécurité renforcée : la villa de Brian Antoni, derrière des grilles en fer forgé.* Gut gesichert: Brian Antonis Villa hinter schmiedeeisernen Gittern.

187 Delighted with her new home: a Cuban lady in the heart of Miami. *Sourire à la nouvelle patrie : une dame cubaine au cœur de Miami.* Lächeln für die neue Heimat: Eine kubanische Lady mitten in Miami.

New York Interiors
Ed. Angelika Taschen, Beate
Wedekind / Flexi-cover, 288 pp. /
€ 14.99 / $ 19.99 / £ 9.99 /
¥ 2.900

Great Escapes North America
Ed. Angelika Taschen, Don
Freeman, Daisann McLane /
Hardcover, 400 pp. / € 29.99 /
$ 39.99 / £ 19.99 / ¥ 5.900

Seaside Style
Ed. Angelika Taschen, Diane
Dorrans Saeks / Flexi-cover,
Icons, 192 pp. / € 6.99 /
$ 9.99 / £ 4.99 / ¥ 1.500

"These books are beautiful objects, well-designed and lucid." —*Le Monde*, Paris, on the ICONS series

"Buy them all and add some pleasure to your life."

African Style
Ed. Angelika Taschen

Alchemy & Mysticism
Alexander Roob

American Indian
Dr. Sonja Schierle

Angels
Gilles Néret

Architecture Now!
Ed. Philip Jodidio

Art Now
Eds. Burkhard Riemschneider,
Uta Grosenick

Atget's Paris
Ed. Hans Christian Adam

Audrey Hepburn
Ed. Paul Duncan

Bamboo Style
Ed. Angelika Taschen

Berlin Style
Ed. Angelika Taschen

Brussels Style
Ed. Angelika Taschen

Cars of the 50s
Ed. Jim Heimann, Tony Thacker

Cars of the 60s
Ed. Jim Heimann, Tony Thacker

Cars of the 70s
Ed. Jim Heimann, Tony Thacker

Chairs
Charlotte & Peter Fiell

Charlie Chaplin
Ed. Paul Duncan

China Style
Ed. Angelika Taschen

Christmas
Ed. Jim Heimann, Steven Heller

Classic Rock Covers
Ed. Michael Ochs

Clint Eastwood
Ed. Paul Duncan

Design Handbook
Charlotte & Peter Fiell

Design of the 20th Century
Charlotte & Peter Fiell

Design for the 21st Century
Charlotte & Peter Fiell

Devils
Gilles Néret

Digital Beauties
Ed. Julius Wiedemann

Robert Doisneau
Ed. Jean-Claude Gautrand

East German Design
Ralf Ulrich / Photos: Ernst Hedler

Egypt Style
Ed. Angelika Taschen

Encyclopaedia Anatomica
Ed. Museo La Specola Florence

M.C. Escher

Fashion
Ed. The Kyoto Costume Institute

Fashion Now!
Ed. Terry Jones, Susie Rushton

Fruit
Ed. George Brookshaw,
Uta Pellgrü-Gagel

HR Giger
HR Giger

Grand Tour
Harry Seidler

Graphic Design
Eds. Charlotte & Peter Fiell

Greece Style
Ed. Angelika Taschen

Halloween
Ed. Jim Heimann, Steven Heller

Havana Style
Ed. Angelika Taschen

Homo Art
Gilles Néret

Hot Rods
Ed. Coco Shinomiya, Tony
Thacker

Hula
Ed. Jim Heimann

Indian Style
Ed. Angelika Taschen

India Bazaar
Samantha Harrison, Bari Kumar

Industrial Design
Charlotte & Peter Fiell

Japanese Beauties
Ed. Alex Gross

Las Vegas
Ed. Jim Heimann,
W. R. Wilkerson III

London Style
Ed. Angelika Taschen

Marilyn Monroe
Ed. Paul Duncan

Marlon Brando
Ed. Paul Duncan

Mexico Style
Ed. Angelika Taschen

Miami Style
Ed. Angelika Taschen

Minimal Style
Ed. Angelika Taschen

Morocco Style
Ed. Angelika Taschen

New York Style
Ed. Angelika Taschen

Orson Welles
Ed. Paul Duncan

Paris Style
Ed. Angelika Taschen

Penguin
Frans Lanting

20th Century Photography
Museum Ludwig Cologne

Photo Icons I
Hans-Michael Koetzle

Photo Icons II
Hans-Michael Koetzle

Pierre et Gilles
Eric Troncy

Provence Style
Ed. Angelika Taschen

Robots & Spaceships
Ed. Teruhisa Kitahara

Safari Style
Ed. Angelika Taschen

Seaside Style
Ed. Angelika Taschen

Signs
Ed. Julius Wiedeman

South African Style
Ed. Angelika Taschen

Starck
Philippe Starck

Surfing
Ed. Jim Heimann

Sweden Style
Ed. Angelika Taschen

Sydney Style
Ed. Angelika Taschen

Tattoos
Ed. Henk Schiffmacher

Tiffany
Jacob Baal-Teshuva

Tiki Style
Sven Kirsten

Tokyo Style
Ed. Angelika Taschen

Tuscany Style
Ed. Angelika Taschen

Valentines
Ed. Jim Heimann,
Steven Heller

Web Design: Best Studios
Ed. Julius Wiedemann

Web Design: E-Commerce
Ed. Julius Wiedemann

Web Design: Flash Sites
Ed. Julius Wiedemann

Web Design: Music Sites
Ed. Julius Wiedemann

Web Design: Portfolios
Ed. Julius Wiedemann

Women Artists
in the 20th and 21st Century
Ed. Uta Grosenick

70s Fashion
Ed. Jim Heimann

ICONS